Ink Converted From Blood

Poem of life!

Dr. Bhaben Choudhury

Made with ❤ on the BookLeaf Publishing Platform
www.bookleafpub.in
www.bookleafpub.com

Dedication

To my parents, whose love and guidance illuminated my
path.
To my readers, whose hearts and minds have resonated
with my words.
And to the entire human family, whose struggles, hopes
and dreams have inspired these poems.

Dr. Bhaben Choudhury

Preface

A Journey Through Life and Emotions: A Review

Dr. Bhaben Choudhury's poetry resonates with a profound blend of human emotions, societal commentary, and personal introspection. His poetic creations are not merely a collection of verses; they are a reflection of the human condition, intricately woven with themes that touch upon personal struggles, collective grief, social inequalities, and spiritual musings. His works delve deep into the realms of nature, humanity, and the trials of modern existence, offering a nuanced perspective on life and its complexities.

Through his words, Dr. Choudhury paints vivid imagery that appeals to the mind and the heart, leaving readers with a sense of introspection and connection. This review seeks to unravel the layers of recurring themes, stylistic devices, and emotional depth that make his poetry profoundly impactful and enduring.

Themes of Pain and Healing:

Pain, healing, and resilience are recurring motifs in Dr. Choudhury's poetry. His poem After the Wait masterfully explores the metaphorical act of severing a wounded hand to prevent the rot from spreading to the entire body. The metaphor speaks to the human condition, emphasizing the courage required to make painful decisions for survival and growth. This act of confronting personal struggles mirrors universal truths about letting go of burdens that impede progress.

The poem juxtaposes personal pain with the grand narrative of human achievement—civilization's rise and space exploration. This contrast not only highlights individual suffering but also underscores the paradox of progress, where humanity's external advancements often coexist with internal turmoil.

Similarly, in In the Pain of My Mother, the poet delves into maternal sacrifice and strength. The imagery of the "lamp burning all night" symbolizes unwavering hope, resilience, and a mother's love as a guiding force in difficult times. Choudhury masterfully captures the duality of anguish and optimism, illustrating how pain can be transformed into fertile ground for new possibilities.

Reflections on Freedom and Confinement:

Freedom and confinement are central themes in Dr. Choudhury's poetic universe. His poem Freedom (At the moment of the 26th Independence Day) critiques the dichotomy between the idealized concept of independence and the grim realities of marginalized communities, such as farmers and laborers. Despite the celebratory promise of liberty, their struggles serve as a stark reminder of societal inequalities, prompting readers to question the true essence of freedom in modern society.

In contrast, Confinement explores the resilience of the human spirit in the face of oppression. Even while trapped, the poet's voice remains unbroken, affirming that truth and hope persist despite silence and adversity. This powerful portrayal of defiance against despair encapsulates the strength that lies within the human soul—a strength that refuses to succumb to the weight of confinement.

Dr. Choudhury's exploration of these themes offers readers a profound understanding of the tensions between external liberty and internal limitations. His work serves as a call to action, urging society to address these contradictions and redefine the meaning of freedom.

Tributes and Loss:

Loss is a theme that finds poignant expression in Dr. Choudhury's poetry. In At the Death of Khagen Mahanta..., the poet mourns the loss of a cultural icon while celebrating his enduring legacy. The imagery of a cuckoo crying and the silence enveloping cultural spaces vividly conveys the collective grief of a community that has lost one of its guiding lights.

Similarly, In Mother's Death and In the Sorrow of Your Absence are deeply personal and heartfelt tributes to maternal love and loss. Through these poems, the poet captures the void left behind by a loved one's absence and the solace drawn from cherished memories. The emotional intensity of these works resonates with readers, reminding them of their own experiences of loss and the strength required to move forward.

Choudhury's ability to weave personal and collective grief into his verses makes his poetry universally relatable. His tributes transcend mere words, becoming a vessel for shared mourning and celebration of life's fleeting beauty.

Social Commentary:

Dr. Choudhury's poetry is deeply rooted in social reality, offering incisive critiques of societal structures and policies. In Honourable Chief Minister, he critiques governmental schemes that, while seemingly benevolent, inadvertently perpetuate dependency and undermine traditional livelihoods. By contrasting the simplicity and self-reliance of rural life with the disillusionment of modern welfare, the poet highlights the unintended consequences of well-meaning policies.

In Liberation, Choudhury channels revolutionary fervor, drawing on historical struggles for equality and justice. References to figures like Mao and the cries of the destitute underscore the intersection of politics and human suffering. The poem serves as a powerful reminder of the sacrifices made for societal transformation and the ongoing fight for a just and equitable world.

These works reveal Choudhury's keen awareness of societal dynamics and his commitment to addressing issues that impact marginalized communities. Through his poetry, he not only critiques but also inspires readers to envision a better future.

Nature and Spirituality:
Nature is a recurring motif in Dr. Choudhury's poetry, often serving as a metaphor for renewal, hope, and resilience. In Glimmer of Dawn, the imagery of birds

sweeping away despair and the light of creation piercing through darkness evokes a profound sense of renewal. This theme is echoed in Consolation, where barren fields and torn earth symbolize despair, while the poet's longing for rain reflects a yearning for rejuvenation and harmony with nature.

Choudhury's connection to the natural world is deeply spiritual, subtly woven into his works. In Feeling, the interplay of moonlight and tangled dreams creates a mystical atmosphere, inviting readers to embark on their own journeys of introspection and self-discovery. His poetry often blurs the lines between the physical and the spiritual, creating a rich tapestry of meaning that resonates on multiple levels.

Through his exploration of nature, Choudhury reminds readers of the interconnectedness of all life and the importance of preserving the delicate balance between humanity and the environment.

Emotional Complexity and Self-Reflection:
Dr. Choudhury's poetry is marked by its emotional complexity and introspective tone. In I Have Lost Myself Within Me, the poet grapples with existential questions, lamenting the suppression of virtue and the prevalence of wickedness. His fading sense of self reflects the inner

conflict faced by individuals navigating an increasingly chaotic world.

Conversely, I Will Return offers a sense of redemption and hope. The poet's determination to break free from despair and cleanse his wounds with his mother's tears illustrates the transformative power of love and resilience. These contrasting themes of despair and renewal underscore the duality of human existence and the enduring quest for meaning.

Choudhury's exploration of identity and inner conflict invites readers to confront their own struggles and embrace the possibility of healing and growth. His introspective approach makes his poetry deeply personal and universally relatable.

Style and Literary Devices:
Dr. Bhaben Choudhury's poetic style is characterized by vivid imagery, metaphorical richness, and rhythmic fluidity. His use of personification, as seen in At the Birth of a Child, where the Himalayas are described as weeping, adds an emotional dimension to his descriptions, making his verses come alive.

Repetition is another hallmark of his style, effectively reinforcing key themes and evoking a sense of urgency.

In In Mother's Death, repetition serves to emphasize the depth of grief and the enduring presence of love in the face of loss.

Choudhury's ability to blend personal experiences with universal truths is one of his greatest strengths. His interplay of light and darkness, hope and despair, and tradition and modernity captures the complexities of human existence with remarkable clarity and depth.

Conclusion:
Dr. Bhaben Choudhury's poetry is a testament to his profound understanding of life's joys and sorrows, triumphs and tribulations. Through his evocative language and insightful commentary, he invites readers to reflect on their own lives and the world around them. His works transcend the boundaries of time and culture, offering timeless insights into the human condition.

Whether exploring themes of pain, freedom, loss, or resilience, Choudhury's poetry leaves an indelible mark on the hearts of his readers. His ability to articulate universal truths with emotional depth and poetic finesse makes him a poet of immense relevance and significance.

In an age where humanity is increasingly disconnected from nature, tradition, and each other, Dr. Choudhury's poetry serves as a beacon of hope and introspection. His verses remind us of the beauty and complexity of life, urging us to confront uncomfortable truths, embrace resilience, and strive for a better future. ▪

Mowsam Hazarika

Writer | Poet | Science Journalist | Sustainability Advocate | Former Director, Assam Seed & Organic Certification Agency | Ex-Joint Director of Agriculture, Assam.

Acknowledgements

Acknowledgments

I would like to express my deepest sense of gratitude to Partha Khargharia, MSc, LLM, who is not only a good hospital management personnel but also a very good human being too. My journey with this book from day one Mr parth help me a lot is correcting not only the sentence but also the words of many poems. His support in last 6 months provide me strong motivation and endurance to successfully accomplish this book of poems. I profusely thank him for his continuous encouragement and valid suggestion while composing the book for final publication
I also express my heartfelt gratitude and earnest regards to Mr Mowsam Hazarika, Poet and writer Retired Director of Agriculture department of Government of Assam being a good critic of my npoems and coming forward to write preface of the book with a critical angle to my poems. His unconditional support in all my tight corners in the course from writing to correcting the poems has v=given me the courage to withstand all the difficult situations and complete my work to make it ready for publication.
Lastly, to acknowledge my family is like thanking

oneself , but I wish to put on my record, the contributions and sacrifices made by my family , specially my daughter Dr Ragini Choudhury, my son Dr Shyam Sekhar Choudhury and my wife Dr Pranita Deka.

Dr Bhaben Choudhury
Writer

2. An Incomplete Poem

(Dedicated to Professor Dr. Dilip Kumar Barua)

Holding your hand, you teach me the alphabet,
I never thought I would write a poem today,
Especially in your presence.
You taught me
Not to be defeated in the battle of life
And to blossom light in the darkness.
You are not unaware;
The first successful surgery of life
Is dedicated in your name,
Without your knowledge.
Today, I realize
With the Gandiva you have crafted in my hands,
I too am proud now,
A victorious soldier.

At the Death of Khagen Mahanta...

At the Birth of a Child

In the distant upward spirals
 Of smoke rings,
 Pulling the veil of mist,
 A colourful circle is drawn.
 Outside, I hear the clamour
 Of the people,
 While a band of deceivers lies asleep.
 Awake today, leaving behind the dreams of two eyes,
 I do not hear the desperate call of the distant four
directions.
 The Himalayas weep, rising high,
 In my courtyard,
 From the fruit of this birth, a child has come.
 And this very child will lead
 The awakened people,
 Leaving behind dreams, they will march forward,
 And the deceivers will be defeated.

My Country, My People

Life floats adrift, coiled in indifference,
And the heart heaves in a hollow thump.
Today, there is no king to feel the pain of the people,
Only jesters pretending to play the part.
Breathing is so hard for me,
Would you lend me a single breath?
Just one breath—
I'm struggling, oh, gasping for air,
Starved of open skies.
To live, I need just one breath from you,
Only a loan—
I promise, I'll return it when better times come,
Your breath, your lifeline.

Confinement

In the net of the makara, the insects waits,
Counting moments until death.
For the sake of freedom,
The makaras have doused the flames.
But,
Even though I am trapped in your net,
I do not count the moment of death.
Because
Even if words are unspoken,
I am not mute.

Consolation

The trees are cut, stripped bare,
In the earth's shame,
Hiding behind the mountain's edge,
Clouds linger silently.
Who will today give me
The news of the rain?
Who will sing today
The melody of the downpour?
The barren fields are crying,
The earth's chest is torn,
Ripped apart with a soft sigh.
Who will today give us solace?

Face

Before entering the surgery room,
 I take a good look at myself,
 Opening my chest and belly,
 I see my heart, stomach, and lungs.
 I keep my face open,

... ...

Clink, clink, clink,
 The sound of the sister's chisel,
 Four operations ready,
 I hold my open face carefully,
 Closing my chest and belly,
 Ah! What a handsome doctor.
 Sister, have you prepped the tools?
After the surgery is done,
 I return to my room.
 I look closely at my open face,
Oh!
How did the morning sun,
Send back the dark clouds?
The whole room is filled
With a foul odor,
In fear, I'm unsettled.

Immediately, I adorn my face
With a flower.
Oh, how beautiful,
The doctor looks.

Feeling

What a feeling it is
To speak of you,
As the moonlight comes, whispering,
Opening the doors of evening.
The moon rises,
Casting its beams
On my tangled dreams,
And on the garden path,
You seem to be unaware,
Have you read the poem,
Written in your name?
Who will announce this tune?
Don't let it slip away,
So brief, yet hard to understand.
There's no heart in it;
I only enjoy talking,
And I love reading your letters.

Feelings 2

I feel like I've found a thread,
 And as soon as I grasp it,
 I realize,
 In the boat of life,
 I am like a traveler from afar.
 Silently, in solitude,
 My futile desires
 Have flown away,
 Wherever they may go,
 Hope alone is the companion of life.
 I know
 That screaming within closed walls
 Brings nothing of value.
 Yet still,
 Feelings awaken like this.

Freedom

(At the moment of the 26th Independence Day)

Freedom!
Just hearing the word makes me tremble,
I forget the sorrows and pains of my heart.
As sadness takes its leave, happiness emerges,
Bringing the fragrance of ripe oranges,
Bringing dreams in colors vivid and bright.
But,
Is the farmer, weary from toil, truly happy,
Who eats just two handfuls a day,
Whose labor makes the earth fruitful?
Is the laborer, worn down by struggle, truly happy,
Who builds and breaks with hands strong,
Whose toil shapes my independent India?

Glimmer of Dawn

Piercing through the darkness,
Pushing away the fragile night,
The glimmer of dawn,
Fills the sky,
With flocks of hopeful birds,
Sweeping away despair.
Open the window by my bedside,
Just look outside
With open eyes.
That's why I've saved
So many words,
Even through my tears.
In the mirror of my memory,
Still shines bright
The essence of creation.

God's Trap

Humans are not weak,
 Mistaking humanity's generosity
As weakness for so long—
God played with man.
The flesh has been cut and torn.
But now, that will not happen again.
Man will play with God,
And for that reason,
The whispers of the home's people
Will become a trap,
Lurking in the calendar of time.

Harsh Reality

A restless world,
An unsettled poet,
The body writhes,
The mind races,
Here and there,
Left, right, forward, back,
Everywhere—
Conflict and strife,
Truth and modernity,
The harsh reality.
With a familiar burden on our shoulders,
Words abound,
We stand captive in hope,
Bound by your words,
Will you return once more
To breathe life into
This garland of poems
You crafted for us?

Honourable Chief Minister

Honourable Chief Minister,
 I too am a village boy,
 My home and fields lie by the river's side.
 In the fields where my father's sweat soaked the soil,
 My mother sowed seeds in the tender earth.
 From the flourishing fields, we'd weave nets, catching
fish.
 Watching the golden fields, my parents counted life's
blessings—
 "Be a good man, my son,
 You must safeguard this land."
 Honourable Chief Minister, I too am a simple village lad.
But I couldn't be that good man,
 Could I even become a true human?
 Honourable Chief Minister,
 Living on your free rice,
 And the few "Arunodoi" coins my mother receives,
 Have left us idle.
 The field lies fallow, abandoned,
 More cows were sold off.
 Someone came, slipped some money into my mother's
hand,

And the next day, a ten-foot wall enclosed our land.
Now, my mother can't even see beyond that tall wall.
And I too am lost, wandering, defeated.
Honourable Chief Minister, I too am a village lad.

*Aunudoi : It is Assam Government Scheme to assist
financially to eligible individual (which is around 27.77
lakhs women). An amount of Rs. 1250.00 monthly is
given to them.*

Hope 1

On Life's Path
Seeing the crooked
 lines of lightning,
 once I thought,
 that is life.
 Today, waking
 from life's half-sleep,
 I hear only
 the echo of a train
 leaving a station behind.

Hope

Let my heart become a monsoon's swollen river,
  its raging waves carrying me away,
  deeper and deeper into the ocean,
  where my mother lies silent and alone.
For today, in this cemetery of a world,
  demons scream, dance, laugh, and sing,
  feasting hungrily on my naked, helpless soul.
Forgive me, Mother, if you can,
  for my powerlessness.

I Have Lost Myself Within Me

Sometimes,
 I lose myself
 within my own being.
 I laugh and laugh,
 when the eternal dies,
 or when the unworthy falls;
 isn't it strange,
 to suppress the virtuous
 while nurturing the wicked?
 Is there no suffering in
 this false existence?
 With hunger in the belly,
 can transformation be possible?
 I see myself slowly
 beginning to fade
 within my own being.

I Shall Not Return

I shall not return, oh mother,
Not at all shall I be able to.
In the silver attire, woven
Into the hair of my mother,
Like the fire of gunpowder,
The warmth of my hands,
Will the lullaby of my mother come?
As soon as the lullaby comes,
I can vanish away,
Without speaking to anyone,
Without calling anyone,
Because
Only the open space of my heart
Has the blood of a demon flowing.
Before the lullaby of my mother is broken,
I want to slip away,
To a distance... to a far distance,
Even if mother calls out,
So that I cannot hear,
To return.
What am I supposed to come back for,
Near my mother,

With my weary heart?

22

I Will Return

I will return
 To my mother's side,
 My mother, frail and weary,
 Lies asleep in silence.
 My hands are stained with blood,
 Dripping from my wounds,
 Yet, I must return.
 To break the chains of my mother's hands,
 To sit in her lap and listen to her lullabies,
 And,
 With her tears, I will wash my hands
 To fly the flag of victory.

Identity

With a glass of sorrow
And a glass of grief,
I sit here
In the midst of darkness,
My heart is empty.
There is nothing to see.
My eyes flutter
In the light,
A dark room—
Quick waves of sound,
In the folds of high music,
The silent bones tremble,
In the melody of the notes,
Identity becomes
Scattered and broken.

In Mother's Death

(At My Mother's Death)

The tears in my eyes are just water,
 Even my own tears are just water.
 With tears pooling in my eyes,
 I bid you farewell, Mother.
While teaching you to take steps,
 I never imagined
 That I would be a traveler
 On your final journey.
You had told me,
 "Never to be defeated in the battle of life,"
 And to live life
 Until the last drop of blood in the body.
But
You have departed,
Smiling, without a word,
Today there is no one to comfort me.
Only your adorned feelings remain
And the boundless strength

To win in the battle of life.

26